Simpson Kalisher
The Alienated Photographer

Simpson Kalisher
The Alienated Photographer

Introduction by Luc Sante

TWO PENNY PRESS, NY

*For America's young
for they will suffer the consequences
or reap the rewards*

PREFACE

The early passions were driven by a need to know.

Photography was a mystery that insisted on being explored, to be touched, but it had to touch me back so that I could understand. Photography was real, it was also metaphysical.

I photographed as much to make pictures as to understand photography.

I wanted to understand my work, my medium, my world and myself at one and the same time.

In the beginning was the rectangle which taught me to see the light whose final lessons were learned in the darkroom.

Lovely, lovely rectangle. There was peace in my rectangle and an immense silence in the darkroom which allowed deep conversations with myself.

All of life was examined that way. I photographed a birth and a death and much in-between. It was there I found the need to re-examine the early stereotypical beautitudes I had been taught.

My rectangle became an inner battleground.

The Talmud lived in the rectangle. The Bible too.
And Karl Marx.

My peace was invaded. The quiet became a din.

SIMPSON KALISHER
Roxbury, Connecticut, 1986

INTRODUCTION

"American life is a billboard," Harold Rosenberg wrote, "individual life in the U. S. includes something nameless that takes place in the weeds behind it." Much of Simpson Kalisher's photographic career has consisted of looking behind that billboard; it is perhaps for this reason that he has chosen to label himself an "alienated photographer." But then you could say that any photographer whose primary business is social observation will perforce be alienated. Alienation is either a precondition of the work or else its consequence.

That is the foundational paradox of street photography. Its practitioner is right there in the middle of the scene, ostensibly a biped like any other, subject to the same conditions of weather and traffic, and yet the photographer's eye is of necessity detached. The photographer's job is to part the veil of pretext—the business or pageantry or camaraderie or regimentation that ostensibly determines the meaning of the tableau—and isolate the specifics, which may well reveal a completely different and perhaps violently contrasting truth. This work separates the photographer from the other actors on the scene even if he or she shares their beliefs. Maybe at length it will chip away at those beliefs. Maybe the discipline imposed by the task will cause the photographer to question the bases of whatever presents itself to his or her eye, and not just the camera's lens. Maybe the eye and the lens will become so interchangeable that the photographer will in a sense be perpetually working. It's a lonely job.

The Alienated Photographer represents a portion of Simpson Kalisher's work, primarily of the 1960s and primarily in and around East Coast cities, especially New York. It is a black-and-white world because that was the photographic convention then—color work did not even begin to achieve respectability until the 1970s. Perhaps the time appears in black-and-white even in memory, but a black-and-white that was somehow crisp and modern then, graphic and objective and pitiless and a thousand miles from the sepia of the dead past. It was far from a static decade; you can feel here the slide from the optimism of the early '60s to the confusion and discord of the decade's end, with a wildly jagged timeline in between. To those born later who are conversant with photography, the scene will appear at least superficially familiar from the works of other photographers, although that is largely circumstantial—they were all drawn by the climate and its overwhelming richness of paradox.

In the city of the 1960s there was still a veneer of inherited formality, trickled down from the nineteenth century but worn wafer-thin by then. Men still wore bowler hats on occasion, for example, under the impression they conveyed distinction rather than doomed haplessness, but then hats in general continued to serve as fictive indicators of status and wealth, even if pretty much everyone could see through their prevarications. The cigar, heraldic emblem of the old plutocracy, garnished the mouths of power-brokers, stockbrokers, ward-heelers, dog-wardens, and garden-variety crooks. Men who were well into the sunset of their years still thought of themselves as boys. Parades remained occasions for tribal display, with atavistic flourishes that had long outlived their purpose. Here you can see all those things crumbling, being eaten by time and change and entropy. A key word of the 1960s was "relevance"; on display here are many of the irrelevancies that brought that notion to the fore.

Also visible in these pictures is the tide of change itself. It is subtle, to be sure. You see it whenever a figure breaks the implied fourth wall and confronts the camera, or whenever anyone registers a genuine and unforced emotion not dictated by social role-play. You see it in an occasional informality that had not yet become the studied and willful informality of subsequent decades but stood for independence and a refusal to serve in the ranks of good behavior. And of course you see it in the kids, who have been buttoned into their suits or uniforms but are bewildered by it all. It is only a matter of time before they first question and then undermine or overthrow the premises of their upbringing—only to substitute another set of premises, but that lies outside the scope of this collection.

Underlying the main story—the transition from an old world to a newer one—is a continuum of loneliness that is the mark of cities in any historical period. Old and young stand alone on the street, looking for something they don't know how to name, and people of all ages are as always herded together in their midtown loneliness—"the lonely crowd" as a book-title of the era had it. A beautiful Great Pyrenees dog, who has established squatter's rights to his fire hydrant, looks loneliest of all, with the particular forlorn abandonment that was to be the hallmark of the half-empty city of the 1970s—as behind him a figure from an earlier era, in his broken-down suit, contemplates the giant question mark of the future.

Simpson Kalisher, our Virgil through this rapidly receding time, gives the impression in every frame of remembering a stricter but richer past while also already perceiving the outline and maybe even the details of the anarchic future, and that perhaps makes him the loneliest of all. He is continually taking a bullet, as it were, for his future viewers, as he confronts thugs and holy joes and uniformed veterans and random citizens who do not wish him well, and we sense that their hostility is exactly the reception we ourselves would get. He does not appear to intrude, exactly—he does not give the impression of climbing into his subjects' protected spaces the way his contemporary Garry Winogrand regularly did—but instead seems to mind his own business about as much as anyone could with a camera in front of his face, so that when he is met with truculence it is surely as undeserved as if our blameless selves were standing in his place.

Kalisher is a versatile photographer who can alter his formal considerations to fit the specifics of what he observes. He is equally at home in sunlight and shadow, and can frame a scene in any of a hundred ways according to the emotional substance at hand—here he is decorous and symmetrical, there bumptious and from-the-hip. His humor is nearly always present, although it is so bone-dry the more literal-minded might sometimes miss it. He does not seem especially romantic here (although his earlier work on railroads gives a quite different impression), and although he can brilliantly dissect a scene so that his eye might be that of an observant alien, seeing things without prejudgment, he can also let you know that he has come upon this sort of thing many, many times before. He appears most jaundiced, interestingly, when he shows the interaction of adults and children—he patently knows what it feels like to be pulled in two separate directions by surly parents, or mauled by an obstreperous aunt when you are not at all in the mood.

There are photographs here that will seem instantly familiar, not because you have seen them before but because they are so perfectly poised and so electrically taut that, like aphorisms, they seem to represent the culmination of a thousand thoughts that were in the air. (Consider the image of the heroic tree-planting, for example, or the two feet protruding beneath the post-office "wanted" board.) Simpson Kalisher is a magnificent photographer of the late twentieth century in America. He makes a very strong case for his alienation, perhaps a necessary condition of his trade, but the results, when gathered together in this volume, express what is perhaps the opposite. These pictures—so unassuming and yet so definitive—declare that they are what we would have seen had we been on the spot. They deliver the truth about a time and a place, lastingly so, with an echo that will continue to resound. This book deserves the widest possible audience.

LUC SANTE

37

AFTERWORD

Photography is difficult only because it is so easy.

We see photographs everywhere, in our daily papers, magazines, on TV, on the web, in museums and art galleries. And in this digital age, with auto focus, auto exposure and auto white balance, we are all photographers.

What are we to make of it? Universally accepted as an art form, how can I (we) distinguish the merely every day from fine art?

There are students of art history who will go on to earn their Masters and PhDs. Some will go on to become museum curators. They will have absorbed history and will organize exhibitions around what they have learned. But once in a while a curator will come along who will find art where all the others have passed it by. In 1967, for example, John Szarkowski mounted an exhibition at MoMA showing the works of Diane Arbus, Lee Friedlander and Garry Winogrand. It changed our sense of what photography was all about. Others will come along some time later to treat us to work that Szarkowski overlooked. What is art? I don't think anyone really knows. We make it up as we go along.

When I decided to make photojournalism my career I was less interested in making art than in making a living. Photojournalism in the late 1940's and early '50's was dominated by *Life* magazine whose picture stories, for the most part, lacked the values I hoped to express in my own work. Then too as I grappled to understand my medium I came to realize that the photographs in the magazines only served as illustrations for the captions which actually told the story.

What of photography as an art form?

Art, I believed, was a form of self expression. And, in my naiveté, I believed that a photograph should be an illustration of what I felt. So, for example, when I saw a Stieglitz photograph of Georgia O'Keeffe's slender hands gracing a wheel on her Ford V-8 convertible, I was prompted to photograph the hands of a black worker washing down one of the white wall tires of my father's 1947 Hudson. It was my first protest photograph.

A photograph, I was beginning to believe, said as much about the subject photographed as it did about the photographer as it did about the medium of photography itself.

My early attempts to execute picture stories followed the format I saw in *Life* which I sought to emulate. The photographs were made in anticipation of the captions which they would illustrate.

But when, in 1950, I had an assignment from a men's adventure magazine to photograph railroad workers in a freight marshalling yard, I performed as a true journalist. I simply captured the action before me. The effort produced the most satisfying photographs I had ever taken. Because the subject did not fit the publisher's sense of adventure, it was never published and the editor, after giving me a bonus, was fired.

Maybe it was my reading of a book of railroad folklore and the emergence of relatively inexpensive tape recorders for home use that prompted my thinking. I wondered if it would be possible to combine photographs with stories told to me by railroad workers. I bought an inexpensive tape recorder and set off to give it a try. *Railroad Men, photographs and collected stories* became my first book and was published in 1961.

In one of the stories in the book a railroad worker talks of the advertisements placed by the American Association of Railroads extolling the working conditions of railroad workers, which the narrator told me was *bad propaganda*. He then went on to give me his version of working conditions, which, to my mind, he should have identified as *good propaganda*. The story in the book was called *Propaganda*.

Propaganda is a neutral word. There are no value judgments to the word propaganda. A person advocating peace is no less a propagandist that someone advocating war. This got me to wondering if it would be possible to create a book that illustrated propaganda in all the ways we see it in the every day, but somehow, through selection and sequencing make my own feelings clear.

It was a difficult book because nothing like this had ever been tried before. Subtlety of meaning has never been a form in photographic literature.

Where to begin?

I first had to overcome my preconception of the lead photograph carried over from the influence of the picture magazines where the lead photograph would dramatically represent the subject and all succeeding photographs would follow logically. No single photograph could explain my intent.

It finally occurred to me that my lead photograph should only make it clear that this was a different kind of book. What better frontispiece photo than a toddler sitting on a restaurant high chair sucking on a pacifier followed with any number of photos that do not appear to relate?

This was going to be fun!

I would select photographs full of meaning and others that were apparently meaningless. I would include photographs that would be relevant to the title, others that were not. Some were funny, others served as allegory and hints of double meanings were still in others. And sequencing would follow visual and graphic cues rather than literal ones so the reader would be prompted to turn the page in anticipation of seeing something new. My hope was that as the reader turned the pages s/he would sense my meaning and even be prompted to go back to the beginning to start all over again.

This became *Propaganda and other Photographs*, my second book, published in 1976.

Jonathan Williams, writing in *Contemporary Photographers*, a book in the St Martins Press'

Contemporary Art Series, wrote "Kalisher's second book, *Propaganda and other Photographs* ……. is another matter: social comment, if you will. Plenty of wit and plenty of vitriol. A dark look at our parlous republic. Dark, but not sour. There is an admirable quiet and solemnity in the way Simpson Kalisher sees things. What makes me again think of Robert Frank is the fact that Kalisher is never some tub-thumping Marxist hack. He is never short on 'pictorial values' though this is getting to be a sin in some critical quarters, particularly amongst those criticasters who can't hit the floor with their hat as regards literary values." Not all reviewers were that understanding.

Now to this newest effort.

Mike Weaver is an author of several books on British and American photography and a former professor of American literature at Oxford University in England. He and I were both invited presenters at a conference at the Center for Creative Photography in Arizona. He was the first presenter and I the last. It was the start of a warm personal friendship.

It was at the end of a long day's social visit with Mike Weaver and Anne Hammond in their suburban Oxford home, after visiting the ancient church where his son was soon to be married, then walking about the local canal and the narrow streets of the town that he asked me to articulate my feelings about photography. The question, after such a relaxed day, took me by surprise. It was such a sharp departure from the relaxed socializing of the day and too big a question to answer easily. To avoid a direct answer, I attempted to deflect the question by answering "Someday I will have to do a book called the alienated photographer." It was an epiphany. I had many differences with the world of photography and now I wondered if it would be possible to create a book that dealt more directly with what I thought and felt. And so the working title *The Alienated Photographer* was born.

But, once again the question arose: where to begin?

I had noted that the photographs of children in *Propaganda and other Photographs* were not seen as being playful. They might even be described as unhappy. Children, I feel, are victims of the adult world which tries to control them by imposing a value system it only professes but cannot really live up to. Children are not fooled, only confused. Children try to understand the world they have been brought into. They try to resolve the contradictions which bring on rebellion, not always with good results.

One photograph that came to mind was of a group of dour faced children in a situation where one would expect to see happy faces. This, I thought would make a great beginning, and it took no time to realize that the following photograph should be of adults in a situation that would serve as a contrast to the first. The goal was to suggest the child's confusing view of the adult world.

The title, *The Alienated Photographer*, has been questioned. I have had a successful career, traveled the world on assignments from a variety of clients, lived in a comfortable home in suburban Connecticut, helped raise four children into well-grounded and talented adults, even had my high speed single engine airplane that allowed me to fly across the country to reach many of my assignment sites. This hardly seems the life of one who claims alienation.

Alienation is a technical term. And while I am not qualified to define it, I can try, at least, to describe it as I understand and felt it.

The most severely alienated find the inconsistencies in modern living intolerable. Hypocrisy, greed and ambition are seen everywhere and the alienated find it impossible to play along. They participate with great difficulty or drop out altogether.

In the opening paragraphs of this essay I said that my original goal as a photographer was to make a living. I had no artistic aspirations. And I wanted to be a photojournalist. But after a number of magazine assignments I came to see the picture story as being no more than soap opera: a young widow left with children to raise on her own (but do not include pictures of the boy friend); sailors on shore leave (for whom I had to get some girls to be their date to satisfy the story's point); a sailor's first trip at sea (and try to make him look animated, which he definitely was not); a typical Vermont village to show the beauty of the fall foliage (taking days to travel through economically depressed towns before finding Peacham, a truly beautiful picturesque place, but hardly typical); a refugee camp in Greece, housing refugees largely from Yugoslavia, Bulgaria and Albania which the editors turned into a typical cold war piece rather than print the story of espionage, counterespionage (and the CIA) which was really going on. I lost interest in photojournalism and became more comfortable with advertising where at least everyone knew the photographs did not represent the truth.

But my interest in photography went beyond making a living. I was taking pictures, developing film and making prints in my preteen years. I read everything I could put my hands on and tried it all. I was fascinated with the process as well as the results. This early fascination served me well as I could make beautiful and convincing photographs which would come to satisfy the needs of my advertising and industrial clients. And it was these photographs that gave me the financial support I sought. But when not on assignment I wandered the streets of my native New York in search of meanings. I did not know where those treks would lead. In my preface I wrote, "I photographed as much to make pictures as to understand photography. I wanted to understand my work, my medium, my world and myself at one and the same time."

In 1978 a gallery in Connecticut invited me to hang my photographs alongside photographs from the files of the Farm Security Administration on loan from the George Eastman House. The FSA photographs depicted scenes from the depression years of the 1930's. Mine, no less social, were not of the poverty stricken, or the disadvantaged, but of everyday scenes taken from my book published a couple of years earlier. The exhibit was titled *Photography as Social Literature*, which also defines my goal in creating books.

A book of photographs can be more than a portfolio. Meanings in a book are not immediately obvious. They evolve. *Propaganda and other Photographs* would not be a book of a single purpose. It would be a commentary on society as well as on photography.

In examining the thousands of photographs taken during my wanderings, I reviewed a myriad of my reactions to what I saw. Some were prompted by a graphic pattern, others by a face, still others by an event and there were still others taken as a reflex reaction to something I could not explain. Then too I had many, many photographs taken for the New York State Council on the Arts. First offered as a grant in 1968, I was asked to create a document of the city of Syracuse, a grant that was renewed three times. With these I still had many more thousands of photographs to review. It is no wonder it took me more than ten years to arrive at my final selection and sequencing.

The Alienated Photographer would not take me that long but its selection and sequencing was not simple either. Where the choice of the frontispiece in the earlier books was a huge obstacle, this one was recognized at once. A book I once read on alienation described its beginnings as coming from confused, conflicting childhood experiences and I knew which photograph expressed that completely. Still there were many variations to the final selection and sequencing. Where the first version had more than 100 prints, the final one was reduced to 63. The discipline was to remove wonderful photographs to adhere to the concept of a book rather than a portfolio.

It is true that some view the photographs in my books as representing the time period in which they were taken or for their photographic qualities. They miss the connections, the allegory, the humor and the social points being made. To them the book is only a portfolio of unconnected scenes. I hope that in time they come to see the larger implications.

SIMPSON KALISHER
New York, 2010

My thanks for the time given and the counsel offered
by Jerry Tolchin and Jesse Kalisher,
as well as corrections of historical fact by Peter C. Bunnell

and for the never ending support of
Gloria Richards

Duotones: Thomas Palmer
palmerwork@cox.net

Publisher Two Penny Press
twopennypress@nyc.rr.com

First printing 2011
ISBN 978-0-578-07134-3

Printed in China